# Connected  Mathematics™

## Number Sense

## Student Edition

Glenda Lappan
James T. Fey
William M. Fitzgerald
Susan N. Friel
Elizabeth Difanis Phillips

*Developed at Michigan State University*

**DALE SEYMOUR PUBLICATIONS®**
MENLO PARK, CALIFORNIA

Connected Mathematics™ was developed at Michigan State University with the support of National Science Foundation Grant No. MDR 9150217.

This project was supported, in part,
by the
**National Science Foundation**
Opinions expressed are those of the authors
and not necessarily those of the Foundation

The Michigan State University authors and administration have agreed that all MSU royalties arising from this publication will be devoted to purposes supported by the Department of Mathematics and the MSU Mathematics Education Enrichment Fund.

This book is published by Dale Seymour Publications®, an imprint of Addison Wesley Longman, Inc.

Dale Seymour Publications
2725 Sand Hill Road
Menlo Park, CA 94025
Customer Service: 800 872-1100

*Managing Editor:* Catherine Anderson
*Project Editor:* Stacey Miceli
*Revision Editor:* James P. McAuliffe
*Production/Manufacturing Director:* Janet Yearian
*Production/Manufacturing Coordinators:* Claire Flaherty, Alan Noyes
*Design Manager:* John F. Kelly
*Photo Editor:* Roberta Spieckerman
*Design:* PCI, San Antonio, TX
*Composition:* London Road Design, Palo Alto, CA
*Electronic Prepress Revision:* A. W. Kingston Publishing Services, Chandler, AZ
*Illustrations:* Pauline Phung, Margaret Copeland, Ray Godfrey
*Cover:* Ray Godfrey

*Photo Acknowledgements:* 5 © Nita Winter/The Image Works; 6 © I. Kostin/The Bettmann Archive; 7 (no roof) © Marc Pesetsky/Reuters/Bettmann; 7 (relief station) © Marc Pesetsky/Reuters/Bettmann; 9 © Ira Schwartz/Reuters/Bettmann; 12 © Stapleton/AP/Wide World Photos; 16 © Stapleton/AP/Wide World Photos; 26 © Roy Ellis/Photo Researchers, Inc.; 29 © Kelley McCall/AP/Wide World Photos; 32 © Photo Researchers, Inc.; 41 © Superstock, Inc.; 54 © Marty Heitner/Superstock, Inc.; 62 © R. M. Collins, III/The Image Works; 67 © Paolo Koch/Rapho/Photo Researchers, Inc.; 68 © NASA

**DALE**
**SEYMOUR**
**PUBLICATIONS®**

Order number 45832
ISBN 1-57232-637-9

3 4 5 6 7 8 9 10-BA-01 00 99 98

# The Connected Mathematics Project Staff

## Project Directors

**James T. Fey**
University of Maryland

**William M. Fitzgerald**
Michigan State University

**Susan N. Friel**
University of North Carolina at Chapel Hill

**Glenda Lappan**
Michigan State University

**Elizabeth Difanis Phillips**
Michigan State University

## Project Manager

**Kathy Burgis**
Michigan State University

## Technical Coordinator

**Judith Martus Miller**
Michigan State University

## Curriculum Development Consultants

**David Ben-Chaim**
Weizmann Institute

**Alex Friedlander**
Weizmann Institute

**Eleanor Geiger**
University of Maryland

**Jane Mitchell**
University of North Carolina at Chapel Hill

**Anthony D. Rickard**
Alma College

## Collaborating Teachers/Writers

**Mary K. Bouck**
Portland, Michigan

**Jacqueline Stewart**
Okemos, Michigan

## Graduate Assistants

**Scott J. Baldridge**
Michigan State University

**Angie S. Eshelman**
Michigan State University

**M. Faaiz Gierdien**
Michigan State University

**Jane M. Keiser**
Indiana University

**Angela S. Krebs**
Michigan State University

**James M. Larson**
Michigan State University

**Ronald Preston**
Indiana University

**Tat Ming Sze**
Michigan State University

**Sarah Theule-Lubienski**
Michigan State University

**Jeffrey J. Wanko**
Michigan State University

## Evaluation Team

**Mark Hoover**
Michigan State University

**Diane V. Lambdin**
Indiana University

**Sandra K. Wilcox**
Michigan State University

**Judith S. Zawojewski**
National-Louis University

## Teacher/Assessment Team

**Kathy Booth**
Waverly, Michigan

**Anita Clark**
Marshall, Michigan

**Julie Faulkner**
Traverse City, Michigan

**Theodore Gardella**
Bloomfield Hills, Michigan

**Yvonne Grant**
Portland, Michigan

**Linda R. Lobue**
Vista, California

**Suzanne McGrath**
Chula Vista, California

**Nancy McIntyre**
Troy, Michigan

**Mary Beth Schmitt**
Traverse City, Michigan

**Linda Walker**
Tallahassee, Florida

## Software Developer

**Richard Burgis**
East Lansing, Michigan

## Development Center Directors

**Nicholas Branca**
San Diego State University

**Dianne Briars**
Pittsburgh Public Schools

**Frances R. Curcio**
New York University

**Perry Lanier**
Michigan State University

**J. Michael Shaughnessy**
Portland State University

**Charles Vonder Embse**
Central Michigan University

# Special thanks to the students and teachers at these pilot schools!

**Baker Demonstration School**
Evanston, Illinois

**Bertha Vos Elementary School**
Traverse City, Michigan

**Blair Elementary School**
Traverse City, Michigan

**Bloomfield Hills Middle School**
Bloomfield Hills, Michigan

**Brownell Elementary School**
Flint, Michigan

**Catlin Gabel School**
Portland, Oregon

**Cherry Knoll Elementary School**
Traverse City, Michigan

**Cobb Middle School**
Tallahassee, Florida

**Courtade Elementary School**
Traverse City, Michigan

**Duke School for Children**
Durham, North Carolina

**DeVeaux Junior High School**
Toledo, Ohio

**East Junior High School**
Traverse City, Michigan

**Eastern Elementary School**
Traverse City, Michigan

**Eastlake Elementary School**
Chula Vista, California

**Eastwood Elementary School**
Sturgis, Michigan

**Elizabeth City Middle School**
Elizabeth City, North Carolina

**Franklinton Elementary School**
Franklinton, North Carolina

**Frick International Studies Academy**
Pittsburgh, Pennsylvania

**Gundry Elementary School**
Flint, Michigan

**Hawkins Elementary School**
Toledo, Ohio

**Hilltop Middle School**
Chula Vista, California

**Holmes Middle School**
Flint, Michigan

**Interlochen Elementary School**
Traverse City, Michigan

**Los Altos Elementary School**
San Diego, California

**Louis Armstrong Middle School**
East Elmhurst, New York

**McTigue Junior High School**
Toledo, Ohio

**National City Middle School**
National City, California

**Norris Elementary School**
Traverse City, Michigan

**Northeast Middle School**
Minneapolis, Minnesota

**Oak Park Elementary School**
Traverse City, Michigan

**Old Mission Elementary School**
Traverse City, Michigan

**Old Orchard Elementary School**
Toledo, Ohio

**Portland Middle School**
Portland, Michigan

**Reizenstein Middle School**
Pittsburgh, Pennsylvania

**Sabin Elementary School**
Traverse City, Michigan

**Shepherd Middle School**
Shepherd, Michigan

**Sturgis Middle School**
Sturgis, Michigan

**Terrell Lane Middle School**
Louisburg, North Carolina

**Tierra del Sol Middle School**
Lakeside, California

**Traverse Heights Elementary School**
Traverse City, Michigan

**University Preparatory Academy**
Seattle, Washington

**Washington Middle School**
Vista, California

**Waverly East Intermediate School**
Lansing, Michigan

**Waverly Middle School**
Lansing, Michigan

**West Junior High School**
Traverse City, Michigan

**Willow Hill Elementary School**
Traverse City, Michigan

# Contents

# Data Around Us

A typical human heart beats about 70 times a minute. How long does it take a heart to beat 1,000,000 times? How long does it take a heart to beat 1,000,000,000 times?

Suppose you were in charge of a relief effort to help 250,000 people who lost their homes in a hurricane. How would you calculate the number of tents and the amount of food and water needed for these people each day?

A news report stated, "Saturday's $43 million lottery Jackpot equals a trail of $1 bills that would stretch 4100 miles, from New York City to San Francisco and back to Glacier National Park in Montana." A dollar bill is about 6 inches long. How many dollar bills are needed to make a trail 1 mile long? How many dollar bills are needed to make a trail 4100 miles long?

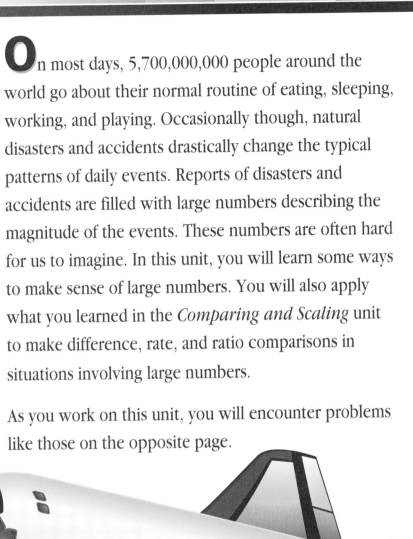

**O**n most days, 5,700,000,000 people around the world go about their normal routine of eating, sleeping, working, and playing. Occasionally though, natural disasters and accidents drastically change the typical patterns of daily events. Reports of disasters and accidents are filled with large numbers describing the magnitude of the events. These numbers are often hard for us to imagine. In this unit, you will learn some ways to make sense of large numbers. You will also apply what you learned in the *Comparing and Scaling* unit to make difference, rate, and ratio comparisons in situations involving large numbers.

As you work on this unit, you will encounter problems like those on the opposite page.

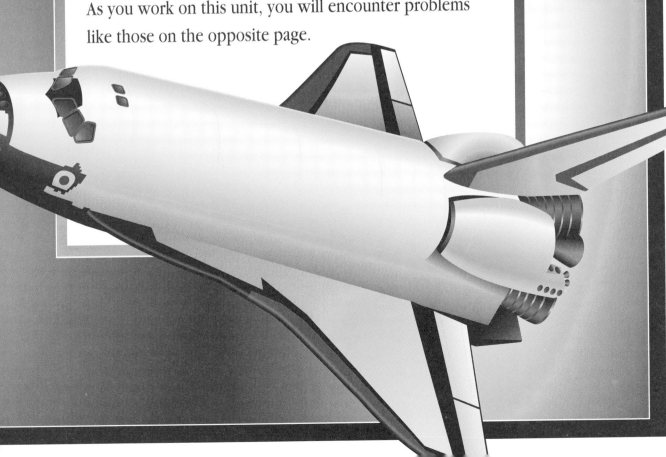

# Mathematical Highlights

In *Data Around Us,* you will learn to make sense of large numbers.

● Developing benchmarks for units of measure helps you make sense of measurements used to describe disasters such as tornadoes, hurricanes, and oil spills.

● Comparing measurements given in news reports to things you are familiar with helps you imagine the magnitude of the measurements.

● Figuring out how many people fit into a 1,000,000-square-centimeter area helps you develop a sense of how big a million is.

● Reading and writing numbers in standard and scientific notation helps you use large numbers more efficiently.

● Rounding values that describe populations, objects, and events allows you to make quick comparisons in situations involving large numbers.

● What you know about ratios, rates, and differences allows you to make comparisons of large numbers and helps you to draw sensible conclusions from given information.

## Using a Calculator

In this unit, you will be able to use your calculator to work quickly and efficiently with the large numbers that represent ratios, quantities of money, or geographical area. As you grow more familiar with large numbers, you will be able to use your calculator to operate with numbers written in scientific notation. As you work on the Connected Mathematics units, you may decide whether using a calculator will help you solve a problem.

# Interpreting Disaster Reports

**W**hen a natural disaster or major accident occurs, news reports are filled with numbers describing the magnitude of the event. In this investigation, you will learn some ways of making sense of such numbers.

## 1.1 Comparing Disasters

To make sense of the numbers in a disaster report, you may want to ask yourself two questions:

*How accurate are the data in this report?*

*How do the data from this disaster compare with data from other disasters or with things I am familiar with?*

Read the following reports, which describe four well-known disasters.

On October 17, 1989, as baseball's World Series was starting in San Francisco, a tremendous earthquake struck the Bay Area, leaving 67 people dead, 3000 people injured, and $10,000,000,000 in property damage. As a result of the earthquake, many major roads and bridges were closed for weeks, paralyzing traffic.

In the early morning of August 24, 1992, Hurricane Andrew roared across the state of Florida from Miami to the Gulf of Mexico. With a top wind speed of 164 miles per hour, it destroyed thousands of homes and businesses, caused $20 billion in property damage, and left 15 people dead and 250,000 homeless before it moved on to Louisiana.

On June 9, 1991, the top of 4795-foot Mount Pinatubo in the Philippine Islands exploded in a volcanic eruption that sent clouds of steam and ash into the atmosphere as high as 80,000 feet. The eruption poured lava as hot as 2000°F down the sides of the mountain. Pinatubo's volcanic ash fell to earth in a 60-mile radius around the mountain. The eruption caused the deaths of 700 people and destroyed 100,000 homes and a U.S. air base.

On April 29, 1986, equipment in several Scandinavian countries detected dangerous levels of radioactivity in the air. The radiation was from a nuclear power plant accident near Chernobyl in the Ukraine. The accident killed at least 34 people, contaminated land for miles around, and left millions of people deeply concerned about their health.

## Problem 1.1

Use the information from the reports above to answer parts A–C.

**A.** Which numbers in the reports are probably very accurate, and which are probably only rough estimates?

**B.** Imagine that you are a journalist writing a story about these four disasters. Write several statements you could use to compare the disasters. For example, you might write, "The 67 deaths caused by the San Francisco Bay Area earthquake of 1989 were more than four times the number of deaths caused by Hurricane Andrew in Florida in 1992."

**C.** Describe the ways you found to compare the disasters.

### ■ Problem 1.1 Follow-Up

How do you think scientists, government officials, and journalists arrive at the numbers in their disaster reports?

## 1.2 Aiding Hurricane Victims

When a natural disaster or tragic accident occurs, people from around the world react quickly, sending clothing, food, medicine, and money. Many people offer their own time and effort to help the injured and homeless and to repair the damage.

When Hurricane Andrew struck south Florida, over 250,000 people were left homeless and without food or water. Relief poured into Florida from all over the United States. Making sure that food and supplies arrived where they were needed was a serious logistical problem.

### Think about this!

**S**uppose you were in charge of a relief effort to help 250,000 people who lost their homes in a hurricane. How would you calculate the number of tents, the amount of food, and the amount of water needed for these people each day?

## Problem 1.2

The United States Marine Corps and the American Red Cross sent relief supplies for families left homeless by the hurricane.

**A.** The U.S. Marines offered tents. Suppose each tent held 18 sleeping cots and covered 500 square feet of ground. Answer parts 1–4, and tell what assumptions you make to answer each question.

  **1.** How many tents would have been needed to take care of all the homeless?

  **2.** How much ground area would have been needed for all these tents?

  **3.** How does the area of one tent compare with the area of your classroom?

  **4.** How many people do you think could sleep in your classroom if a disaster struck your town? How many people do you think could sleep in your school?

**B.** The Red Cross provided cots, blankets, food, and water for the tent city and other shelters. They set up 126 feeding stations and 230 shelters. Answer parts 1–4, and tell what assumptions you make to answer each question.

  **1.** If each person received at least one meal a day, about how many meals did each feeding station have to provide each day?

  **2.** About how many students are served in your school's cafeteria each day?

  **3.** How many cafeterias like your school's would be needed to serve 250,000 people?

  **4.** The shelters housed a total of 85,154 people. What was the average number of people per shelter?

### ■ Problem 1.2 Follow-Up

The Red Cross reported serving 4,779,161 meals during the relief effort in Florida. How do you think this number was determined?

As you work on these ACE questions, use your calculator whenever you need it.

# Applications

In 1–5, use the information from these reports of well-known American disasters.

*The Blizzard of 1888*   From March 11 through March 14 of 1888, a huge blizzard covered the eastern United States with as much as 5 feet of snow. The storm caused 400 deaths and $20 million in damage.

*The Tropical Storm of 1972*   In June of 1972, Tropical Storm Agnes moved up the East Coast of the United States, causing flash floods that killed 129 people, left 115,000 people homeless, and caused $3.5 billion of damage.

*The Floods of 1993*   From June through August of 1993, heavy rains in the midwestern United States led to flooding that caused 50 deaths, left 70,000 people homeless, and damaged $12 billion worth of crops and buildings.

**1.** Which numbers in these reports are probably very accurate, and which are probably only rough estimates?

**2.** Which disaster caused the greatest financial loss? How did you decide?

**3.** Compare the loss of life from the Blizzard of 1888 with the loss of life from Tropical Storm Agnes.

**4.** Compare the loss of life from Tropical Storm Agnes with the loss of life from the Midwest floods of 1993.

**5.** Compare the loss of life from the Blizzard of 1888 with the loss of life from the Midwest floods of 1993.

# Connections

**6.** If the floor of a Marine hurricane-relief tent is a rectangle with an area of 500 square feet, what might the dimensions of the tent be?

**7.** On October 8, 1871, a wildfire destroyed the town of Peshtigo, Wisconsin, and much of the surrounding forest. More than 1200 people were killed, and 2 billion trees were burned.

    **a.** What method might have been used to estimate the number of trees burned?

    **b.** What similar estimation problems have you encountered in other Connected Mathematics units?

# Extensions

**8.** Below are scale drawings of a cot and the floor of a Marine tent.

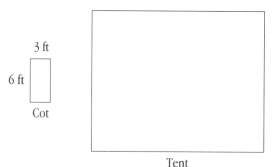

    **a.** How many cots could fit in a tent?

    **b.** If you were in charge of setting up the cots, how many cots would you put in each tent? How would you arrange the cots? Draw a diagram to illustrate your answer.

**9.** Read about great disasters in a world almanac.

    **a.** Which disaster do you believe was the worst of all time? Explain your choice.

    **b.** Make up a math problem about the disaster you chose for part a.

# Mathematical Reflections

In this investigation, you looked at reports of natural disasters and accidents. You thought about how accurate the numbers in these reports might be and considered how the numbers might have been obtained. You also looked for ways to compare one disaster with another. These questions will help you summarize what you have learned:

**1** What clues can help you decide whether a number is accurate or only a rough estimate?

**2** In what ways can you compare data describing damage for one disaster with data describing damage for another disaster?

Think about your answers to these questions, discuss your ideas with other students and your teacher, and then write a summary of your findings in your journal.

# Measuring Oil Spills

**O**ur modern world depends on crude oil for energy and other products. As a result, huge tankers travel the world's oceans carrying oil from where it is found to where it is used. Unfortunately, some of these tankers have accidents and spill their sticky cargo on waters, beaches, and sea animals.

News reports of oil spills usually try to communicate the amount of oil spilled. Such reports may tell how many barrels were spilled, or they may give the surface area or volume of the spill. What do you think would be the best way to describe the size of an oil spill?

## 2.1 Describing an Oil Spill

Numbers are essential in reporting the size and effects of oil spills and in preparing for cleanup actions. To see how important numbers are, try reading this "censored" story about a famous oil spill.

> Shortly after **A** on **B** a giant oil tanker left Valdez, Alaska, with a load of **C** of crude oil from the Alaskan pipeline. To avoid icebergs, the ship took a course about **D** out of the normal shipping channel. Unfortunately, less than **E** later the ship ran aground on the underwater Bligh Reef. The rocks of the reef tore a **F** gash in the tanker's hull, and **G** of crude oil spilled onto the surface of Prince William Sound. For weeks, the world watched closely as the *Exxon Valdez* oil spill became an environmental disaster, despite extensive efforts to contain and clean up the oil. The spill gradually spread to form an oil slick, covering **H** of water and killing **I** sea otters and **J** birds. The cleanup engaged **K** of boats and workers, who struggled against the cold of **L** water and air temperatures. The cleanup cost was over **M**, including **N** for wildlife rescue alone.

## Problem 2.1

Match each lettered blank in the story with the correct measurement or range of numbers from the list below. Be prepared to explain your reasons for each choice.

| | | |
|---|---|---|
| 800 square miles | 10,080,000 gallons | $41 million |
| 2000 to 3000 | 600-foot | 2 miles |
| 40° Fahrenheit | 150 centimeters | 90,000 to 300,000 |
| $2 billion | March 24, 1989 | 52,000,000 gallons |
| thousands | 3 hours | 9:00 P.M. |

### ■ Problem 2.1 Follow-Up

The numbers and measurements in Problem 2.1 describe attributes such as area, volume, and time. For example, "800 square miles" describes the area of the oil slick. You can tell that 800 square miles is an area measurement by looking at the units. Square miles are units of area. For parts A–N, describe what is being measured—for example, area, length, volume, weight, or time.

## 2.2 Finding Benchmarks for Units of Measure

The news report in Problem 2.1 gives measurements of time, length, area, volume, temperature, money, population, and so on. These measurements are given in two parts: a *count* and a *unit of measure.* The count tells how many units of measure are being considered. For example, 10,080,000 gallons is the volume of oil spilled. The unit of measure is gallons, and the count is 10,080,000.

To understand disaster reports in which large numbers are used, you need a sense of the size of different units of measure. You also need a sense of what large numbers "look like." For example, to imagine 10,080,000 gallons, you need a sense of "how big" a gallon is and of "how many" 10,080,000 is.

In this problem, you will develop some *benchmarks* to help you think about units of measure. In the United States, we use two systems of measurement. The *customary system* includes inches, gallons, and pounds. The *metric system* includes meters, liters, and grams.

---

### Problem 2.2

This problem will help to refresh your memory of customary and metric units.

**A.** In your group, think of as many units of length, area, volume, weight or mass, temperature, and time as you can. Record each unit on a stick-on note. Be sure to think of both customary and metric units.

**B.** Group the units by the attributes they measure. Put all the units of length together, all the units of area together, and so on.

**C.** For each unit, try to think of something familiar that is about the size of 1 unit. For example, a sheet of notebook paper is about 1 foot long. A single-serving container of yogurt holds about 1 cup. Add each example to the stick-on note with the unit name. You can use these examples as *benchmarks* to help you imagine the size of something when a measurement is given.

---

## Problem 2.2 Follow-Up

Sometimes it is convenient to know the relationship between customary and metric units of measure. The following are some common *conversions:*

1 inch = 2.54 centimeters      1 gallon ≈ 3.785 liters      1 pound ≈ 0.454 kilogram

**1. a.** Find or think of an object whose length is commonly measured in customary units. Give the length of the object in customary units, and then convert the length to metric units.

  **b.** Find or think of an object whose length is commonly measured in metric units. Give the length of the object in metric units, and then convert the length to customary units.

**2. a.** Find or think of an object whose volume is commonly measured in customary units. Give the volume of the object in customary units, and then convert the volume to metric units.

  **b.** Find or think of an object whose volume is commonly measured in metric units. Give the volume of the object in metric units, and then convert the volume to customary units.

### Did you know?

Ounces and pounds are measures of weight. *Weight* is the force with which an object is attracted toward Earth (or some other body). Grams and kilograms are measures of mass. *Mass* is a measure of the amount of material an object contains. If you stood on the Moon, you would have the same mass that you have on Earth. However, since the gravitational pull of the Moon is weaker than that of Earth, you would weigh less on the Moon than you do on Earth. For measurements made on Earth, the distinction between mass and weight is not critical, and the terms are often used interchangeably.

**3. a.** Find or think of an object whose weight is commonly measured in customary units. Give the weight of the object in customary units, and then convert this measurement to metric units.

  **b.** Find or think of an object whose mass is commonly measured in metric units. Give the mass of the object in metric units, and then convert this measurement to customary units.

**4.** Find three items in your home or school that are labeled with both customary and metric units.

## 2.3 Developing a Sense of Large Numbers

You can imagine what a gallon of oil looks like, but can you imagine 10,080,000 gallons spread over 800 square miles of Prince William Sound? You have a sense of how long a foot is, but can you picture a 600-foot gash in the hull of an oil tanker? You know the value of $1, but can you imagine the value of the $41 million spent rescuing wildlife from the *Exxon Valdez* oil spill?

One way to understand measurements with large numbers is to find something familiar that is the same size. For example, Los Angeles and New York City have a combined land area of just about 800 square miles. The *Exxon Valdez* oil slick would have nearly covered those two cities.

Another way to make sense of measurements with large numbers is to think about copies of something familiar. For example, an American football field is 300 feet long (without the end zones). The gash in the *Exxon Valdez* was as long as two football fields. Operating America's public schools costs an average of $4500 per student each year. The money spent on the *Exxon Valdez* wildlife rescue is equal to the cost of school for more than 9000 students—or all the seventh graders in Alaska!

### Did you know?

The immediate impact of the *Exxon Valdez* oil spill on the marine wildlife in coastal Alaska was tremendous. Within two months of the disaster, cleanup crews had retrieved over 35,000 dead birds from the state's oily shorelines. Biologists estimate that a total of about 250,000 birds were killed by the spill. One species, the marbled murrelet, lost an amazing 30 percent of its native population. Fortunately, as the Alaskan ecosystem slowly heals, seabird colonies have been returning to their earlier population levels.

## Problem 2.3

In parts A–G, facts about the *Exxon Valdez* disaster are given. Imagine you are a newspaper reporter assigned to the story. Use your own ideas or the hints given to write statements communicating each fact in a way that would be easy for your readers to understand.

**A.** *The* Exxon Valdez *spilled 10,080,000 gallons of crude oil.*
Hint: An Olympic-size swimming pool holds about 500,000 gallons of water. How many such pools could be filled with the 10,080,000 gallons of oil?

**B.** *The tanker strayed about 2 miles out of the usual shipping channel.*
Hint: What places in your area are about 2 miles apart?

**C.** *The water and air temperatures during the oil spill cleanup were about 40° Fahrenheit.*
Hint: When, if ever, do the water and air temperatures in your area reach these temperatures? Do you go swimming then?

**D.** *The tanker ran aground on Bligh Reef less than 3 hours after it left port.*
Hint: What familiar events last about 3 hours?

**E.** *The oil spill killed 90,000 to 300,000 seabirds.*
Hint: Consult an almanac or atlas to find cities or towns in your state with human populations about this size.

**F.** *The entire cleanup operation cost $2,000,000,000.*
Hint: In the United States, the mean annual pay for workers is about $25,000. How many annual salaries could be paid from the cleanup cost of the oil spill?

**G.** *The oil slick eventually covered 800 square miles of the ocean's surface.*
Hint: 1 mile is 5280 feet, so 1 square mile is $5280 \times 5280 = 27,878,400$ square feet. Estimate the area of your classroom floor. Then, figure out how many such classroom floors it would take to cover 1 square mile and to cover the 800-square-mile oil slick.

## ■ Problem 2.3 Follow-Up

The *Exxon Valdez* oil tanker was 987 feet long. You can get a sense of this length by imagining a "human chain."

**1.** Make an estimate of the arm span, in feet, of a typical seventh grader. Figure out how many seventh graders it would take to stretch out in a line as long as the *Exxon Valdez*.

**2.** Would the chain require more students than are in your class? Would it require more students than are in your school?

**3.** Would this chain fit in the hall of your school? Would it fit across the football field or soccer field?

As you work on these ACE questions, use your calculator whenever you need it.

# Applications

In 1–6, use the following information: On May 18, 1980, Mount St. Helens, a volcano in southwestern Washington, erupted with a blast of hot gas and rock that devastated more than **150,000 acres** of prime timberland and sent a mushroom cloud of ash **90,000 feet** into the atmosphere and then around the world. The blast triggered the largest landslide in recorded history—**4 billion cubic yards** of shattered rock poured down the mountainside at a speed of **17,600 feet per minute.** The Mount St. Helens eruption killed **60 people** and caused an estimated **$970 million** in damage. When the main eruption was over, the mountain had lost **1313 feet** from its original height of **9677 feet.**

**1.** Tell which of the boldface measurements are measures of the given attribute.

    **a.** length     **b.** area     **c.** volume     **d.** weight or mass

    **e.** money     **f.** speed     **g.** temperature     **h.** population

**2.** The Washington Monument is 550 feet tall. How many such monuments would be needed to make a tower reaching to the top of the Mount St. Helens ash cloud?

**3.** Glenn Robinson, the Milwaukee Bucks basketball star, earns about $6 million per year. How many years of his salary would be needed to pay for the damage from the Mount St. Helens eruption?

**4.** The median annual salary per worker in the United States in 1983 was about $16,300. About how many such salaries would it take to pay for the damage from the Mount St. Helens eruption?

**5.** The playing field in a major league baseball park covers about 2 acres of land. How many such fields would it take to cover the timberland destroyed by the Mount St. Helens eruption?

**6.** Use the given facts as benchmark data to write statements for a news report describing the size and effects of the Mount St. Helens eruption.

    **a.** The Louisiana Superdome is the largest sports arena in the world. It covers 13 acres and reaches a height of about 350 feet.

    **b.** A car traveling 65 miles per hour moves 5720 feet per minute.

    **c.** Sixty-seven deaths were caused by the San Francisco earthquake of October 17, 1989.

**7.** An offshore oil platform, Hibernia, is being built 200 miles off the coast of Newfoundland. It will weigh 600,000 tons, making it the heaviest such platform in the world. Develop a benchmark to help you make sense of the weight of this platform.

# Connections

**8.** Tell what customary and metric units you could use to measure the following things. For example, for a television set, you could measure the length, width, or diagonal of the screen in inches or centimeters; you could measure the weight or mass in pounds or kilograms; and you could measure the area of the screen in square inches or square centimeters.

    **a.** a car           **b.** a contact lens

    **c.** a trip from Boston to Seattle           **d.** a house or an apartment

    **e.** the water used in your school each day

**9.** When oil began leaking from the *Exxon Valdez*, cleanup teams tried to contain the spill by surrounding it with floating booms. Before the slick could be contained, the oil spread too far for the supply of boom sections.

    **a.** Suppose you have 20,000 meters of boom sections to arrange in the shape of a rectangle. Of all the rectangles you could make from the boom sections, which rectangle would have the greatest area? Give the dimensions and the area of the rectangle.

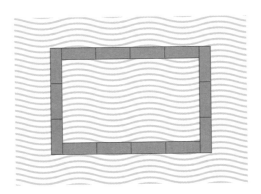

    **b.** Suppose you can arrange 20,000 meters of flexible boom sections in any shape you choose. Which shape could contain the greatest oil slick area?

# Extensions

In 10 and 11, use the following information: In terms of gallons of oil spilled, there have been spills larger than the *Exxon Valdez* disaster. On July 19, 1979, two tankers collided near the islands of Trinidad and Tobago, releasing 88,200,000 gallons of crude oil into the Caribbean Sea. On June 3, 1979, an oil well in the Gulf of Mexico exploded and spilled 180,000,000 gallons of crude oil before it was capped.

**10.** Compare the *Exxon Valdez* disaster with these two spills.

**11.** If you were writing a news report on these spills, what other measures of damage would you want to include?

# Mathematical Reflections

In this investigation, you reviewed customary and metric units of measure. You also practiced some useful strategies for making sense of disaster reports that include large numbers and many different units. These questions will help you summarize what you have learned:

1. What are some common units for measuring length, area, volume, weight or mass, temperature, and time?

2. What familiar things could you use as benchmarks to explain to someone the sizes of the units you listed in question 1? Select one or two units of measure for each type of measurement (length, area, volume, and so on), and give an example of a benchmark for each.

3. What are some strategies you can use to better understand the size of something that is expressed by a measurement with a very large number?

Think about your answers to these questions, discuss your ideas with other students and your teacher, and then write a summary of your findings in your journal.

# INVESTIGATION

# Comparing Large Numbers

**Y**ou have seen that the numbers used to report the size of natural disasters and accidents are often very large. Hurricane Andrew caused $20 billion in property damage; the *Exxon Valdez* oil slick covered about 22,300,000,000 square feet of ocean surface; and the Mount St. Helens eruption blasted 4 billion cubic yards of rock off the top of the mountain. To solve problems about situations like these and to discuss your results with others, you need to know how to write and read large numbers.

The standard notation for writing numbers involves ten digits—0, 1, 2, 3, 4, 5, 6, 7, 8, and 9—and a *place-value system*. To write and read numbers greater than 999, we group the places into clusters of three.

| trillions | | | billions | | | millions | | | thousands | | | ones | | |
|---|---|---|---|---|---|---|---|---|---|---|---|---|---|---|
| 4 | 3 | 6, | 5 | 7 | 2, | 8 | 9 | 1, | 7 | 5 | 3, | 2 | 5 | 4 |
| hundred trillions | ten trillions | trillions | hundred billions | ten billions | billions | hundred millions | ten millions | millions | hundred thousands | ten thousands | thousands | hundreds | tens | ones |

The number 436,572,891,753,254 is read "four hundred thirty-six *trillion,* five hundred seventy-two *billion,* eight hundred ninety-one *million,* seven hundred fifty-three *thousand,* two hundred fifty-four." Notice that in this number the digit 2 appears in two places. In one place, it stands for two billion; in the other place, it stands for two hundred.

**Playing Dialing Digits**

You can test your skill in reading, writing, and comparing numbers by playing the Dialing Digits game.

### Rules for Dialing Digits

Dialing Digits is played by two or more players or teams.

*Materials*
- Pencils
- Dialing Digits spinner
- Dialing Digits game cards (1 per player)

On the Dialing Digits game card, the blanks for each game represent place values for a nine-digit number.

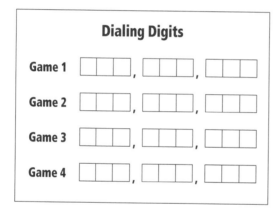
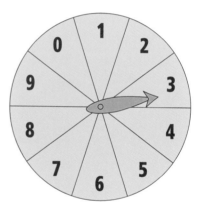

*Directions*
- Players take turns spinning the spinner. After each spin, each player must write the digit spun in one of the empty blanks for that game. Players should keep their game cards hidden from each other until the end of the game.
- The game proceeds until all the blanks have been filled. The player that has placed the digits to make the greatest number wins. However, before earning the win, the player must correctly read the number that has been produced.

### Problem 3.1

Play Dialing Digits several times with different opponents. Record any strategies you find that help you win.

## Problem 3.1 Follow-Up

You can vary Dialing Digits to make it more challenging. Here are two variations:

- Play two rounds of the game, and have each player add his or her numbers for the two rounds. The player with the greatest sum wins.
- Play two rounds of the game, and have each player subtract the number for round 2 from the number for round 1. The team with the greatest difference wins.

Play Dialing Digits again, using one of these variations. Describe a strategy for winning.

## 3.2  Getting Things in Order

You have seen that reports of natural disasters often involve large numbers. Large numbers also occur frequently in population data. The table below shows 1992 populations of the 20 largest metropolitan areas in the United States. A *metropolitan area* consists of a central city and smaller surrounding communities.

| Metropolitan area | Population |
|---|---|
| Atlanta | 2,959,950 |
| Boston | 5,455,403 |
| Chicago | 8,239,820 |
| Cleveland | 2,859,644 |
| Dallas | 4,037,282 |
| Detroit | 5,187,171 |
| Houston | 3,731,131 |
| Los Angeles | 14,531,529 |
| Miami | 3,192,582 |
| Minneapolis | 2,538,834 |
| New York City | 19,549,649 |
| Philadelphia | 5,892,937 |
| Phoenix | 2,238,480 |
| Pittsburgh | 2,394,811 |
| St. Louis | 2,492,525 |
| San Diego | 2,498,016 |
| San Francisco | 6,253,311 |
| Seattle | 2,970,328 |
| Tampa | 2,067,959 |
| Washington, D.C. | 6,727,050 |

Source: U.S. Bureau of the Census, as reported in *The World Almanac and Book of Facts 1996.* Ed. Robert Famighetti. Mahwa, New Jersey: Funk and Wagnalls, 1995.

## Problem 3.2

The census data are given in alphabetical order, but it is often interesting and important to look at *ranking* by size. An increase in population can bring greater political and economic power to an area.

**A.** Order the 20 metropolitan areas from most populated to least populated.

**B.** Describe some ways you could compare the populations of these metropolitan areas.

**C.** Locate each of the 20 metropolitan areas on the U.S. map on Labsheet 3.2. Look for interesting patterns in the locations of these areas.

    **1.** What geographic factors seem to lead to large population centers?

    **2.** How do you think the locations of these large metropolitan areas affect national and state government and business decisions?

### ■ Problem 3.2 Follow-Up

**1.** The table on the next page shows the population of the major city in each metropolitan area. List the cities in order from most populated to least populated.

**2.** Compare the ranking for the cities to the ranking for the metropolitan areas. Give some possible reasons for any differences you find.

| Metropolitan area | Population of metropolitan area | Population of city |
|---|---|---|
| Atlanta | 2,959,950 | 393,929 |
| Boston | 5,455,403 | 574,283 |
| Chicago | 8,239,820 | 2,783,726 |
| Cleveland | 2,859,644 | 505,616 |
| Dallas | 4,037,282 | 1,007,618 |
| Detroit | 5,187,171 | 1,027,974 |
| Houston | 3,731,131 | 1,629,902 |
| Los Angeles | 14,531,529 | 3,485,557 |
| Miami | 3,192,582 | 358,648 |
| Minneapolis | 2,538,834 | 368,383 |
| New York City | 19,549,649 | 7,322,564 |
| Philadelphia | 5,892,937 | 1,585,577 |
| Phoenix | 2,238,480 | 983,403 |
| Pittsburgh | 2,394,811 | 369,879 |
| St. Louis | 2,492,525 | 396,685 |
| San Diego | 2,498,016 | 1,110,554 |
| San Francisco | 6,253,311 | 723,959 |
| Seattle | 2,970,328 | 516,259 |
| Tampa | 2,067,959 | 280,015 |
| Washington, D.C. | 6,727,050 | 606,900 |

Source: U.S. Bureau of the Census, as reported in *The World Almanac and Book of Facts 1996.* Ed. Robert Famighetti. Mahwa, New Jersey: Funk and Wagnalls, 1995.

## Did you know?

With more than half the state's automobile and human populations, New York City has its share of cleaning to do. While people may complain about how dirty the city is, the streets today are spotless compared to 150 years ago. Before the first sewer systems were built during the nineteenth century, New York City streets were so filthy that herds of abandoned farm hogs roamed the city, eating the trash that piled up along the roadside. During his visit to the city in 1842, British author Charles Dickens joked that New Yorkers ought to "take care of the pigs, for they are the city scavengers." Today, structural engineers face the difficult task of renovating old-fashioned sewer systems without disturbing the bustling businesses of America's largest city.

## 3.3 Rounding Numbers

The census data in Problem 3.2 are given as exact counts, but since exact populations are difficult to calculate and change daily, populations are often given as rounded figures. For example, the population of the Los Angeles metropolitan area might be rounded as shown:

| | |
|---|---|
| Actual count (1992) | 14,531,529 |
| Rounded to the nearest ten million | 10,000,000 |
| Rounded to the nearest million | 15,000,000 |
| Rounded to the nearest hundred thousand | 14,500,000 |

By using rounded numbers, you can give a general idea of size without claiming exactness. And, most people find it easier to think about and compare numbers with fewer non-zero digits. When you round a number, you need to consider the situation in order to decide how accurate the rounded number should be.

### Problem 3.3

In 1990, the population of the United States was reported to be 248,709,873. Here are four possible roundings of this number:

200,000,000          250,000,000          249,000,000          248,700,000

**A.** The population of the world is about 5.7 billion. Which of the above roundings would you use if you wanted to compare the population of the United States with the population of the world? Give reasons for your choice.

**B.** The population of India is about 1 billion. Which rounding would you use if you wanted to compare the population of the United States with the population of India? Give reasons for your choice.

**C.** In 1980, the population of the United States was about 226,000,000. Which rounding would you use if you wanted to compare the 1990 U.S. population with this 1980 population figure? Give reasons for your choice.

### ■ Problem 3.3 Follow-Up

Look again at the list of the 20 largest metropolitan areas. Round these population figures in a way that makes sense to you. Explain your reasoning. Do your roundings preserve the original ranking? Why or why not?

**Comparing Hog Populations**

In areas with large populations of people or animals, finding ways to dispose of waste can be a problem. Any area must deal with the storage, treatment, and disposal of garbage and hazardous chemical wastes. Areas with industries involving great numbers of animals must also deal with the treatment and disposal of animal wastes.

## Did you know?

In 1995, at a hog farm in northern Onslow County, North Carolina, the walls of an 8-acre wastewater lagoon collapsed. Within an hour, 25 million gallons of raw hog waste had poured through a 25-foot-wide breech in the 12-foot wall into a nearby river. Over the next few days, the wastewater swirled downstream, smothering and suffocating more than 3500 fish.

Hog farming is an important business in North Carolina. In fact, one area of the state, shown in dark orange on the map below, is known as the "hog belt."

The table below gives data for the 15 North Carolina counties with the greatest 1993 hog populations. For each county, the table gives the 1993 hog population, the percent growth from 1983 to 1993, and the number of hogs per square mile.

| County | 1993 hog population | Growth from 1983 | Hogs per square mile |
|--------|--------------------|------------------|----------------------|
| Sampson | 1,152,000 | 363% | 1218 |
| Duplin | 1,041,000 | 349% | 1273 |
| Wayne | 333,000 | 265% | 603 |
| Bladen | 271,000 | 1178% | 310 |
| Greene | 231,000 | 82% | 870 |
| Pitt | 193,000 | 128% | 297 |
| Lenoir | 159,000 | 312% | 399 |
| Johnston | 129,000 | 61% | 163 |
| Robeson | 124,000 | 81% | 131 |
| Onslow | 115,000 | 261% | 150 |
| Jones | 105,000 | 999% | 223 |
| Beaufort | 103,000 | 51% | 125 |
| Pender | 97,000 | 588% | 111 |
| Halifax | 82,000 | 18% | 113 |
| Northampton | 81,000 | 53% | 151 |

Source: U.S. Department of Agriculture, as reported in the *Raleigh News and Observer,* 19–26 February 1995.

## Problem 3.4

**A.** Write at least three statements comparing the hog data for Johnston County with the hog data for Bladen County.

**B.** Choose two different pairs of counties from the table. For each pair, write at least three statements comparing the hog data for the two counties.

### ■ Problem 3.4 Follow-Up

Find the mean and median of the 1993 hog populations for the 15 counties. How do the mean and median compare? If they are different, explain why. How do the mean and median help in describing the hog populations of these counties?

As you work on these ACE questions, use your calculator whenever you need it.

# Applications

In 1–7, use the following table, which gives data regarding U.S. casualties in major wars from the Revolutionary War to the Persian Gulf War. A dash (—) indicates that the information is not available.

| War | People serving | Battle deaths | Other deaths | Battle injuries | Total casualties |
|---|---|---|---|---|---|
| Revolutionary War | 184,000 to 250,000 | 6824 | 18,500 | 8445 | 33,769 |
| War of 1812 | 286,730 | 2260 | — | 4505 | 6765 |
| Mexican War | 78,718 | 1733 | 11,550 | 4152 | 17,435 |
| Civil War (Union) | 2,213,363 | 140,414 | 224,097 | 281,881 | 646,392 |
| Civil War (Confederate) | 600,000 to 1,500,000 | 74,524 | 59,297 | — | 133,821 |
| Spanish-American War | 306,760 | 385 | 2061 | 1662 | 4108 |
| World War I | 4,743,826 | 53,513 | 63,195 | 204,002 | 320,710 |
| World War II | 16,353,659 | 292,131 | 115,185 | 670,846 | 1,078,162 |
| Korean War | 5,764,143 | 33,651 | — | 103,284 | 136,939 |
| Vietnam War | 8,744,000 | 47,369 | 10,799 | 153,303 | 211,471 |
| Persian Gulf War | 467,539 | 148 | 145 | 467 | 760 |

Source: Revolutionary War: *The Toll of Independence*, Ed. Howard H. Peckham, Chicago: University of Chicago Press, 1974. All other wars: U.S. Department of Defense, as reported in *The World Almanac and Book of Facts 1996*. Ed. Robert Famighetti. Mahwa, New Jersey: Funk and Wagnalls, 1995.

**1.** In World War II, 16,353,659 Americans served in the fighting forces. Write this number in words.

**2.** In the Civil War, 2,213,363 people served in the Union army. Write this number in words.

**3.** Rank the ten wars from greatest to least in terms of the number of people serving. (Combine Union and Confederate data for the Civil War.)

**4.** Rank the wars from greatest to least in terms of the total number of casualties. (Combine Union and Confederate data for the Civil War.)

**5. a.** For each war, what percent of the number of people serving were casualties? (Combine Union and Confederate data for the Civil War.)

**b.** Using the percents you found in part a, rank the wars from the greatest percent of casualties to the least percent of casualties.

**c.** How does this ranking compare with the rankings you made in questions 3 and 4? Give possible reasons for any differences in the rankings.

**6. a.** For each war, find the total number of deaths.

**b.** Round your answers from part a to the nearest thousand.

**7.** Find the five greatest numbers in the table, and round each to the nearest hundred thousand.

# Connections

**8.** Suppose you play a two-digit version of Dialing Digits (from Problem 3.1).

**a.** What is the greatest number you could create?

**b.** What is the probability of getting this number on two spins?

**c.** If the result of the first spin is recorded in the first blank, what is the probability of getting a two-digit number in the forties?

**9.** Most of the war data used in questions 1–7 appear to be given as exact counts.

**a.** Which numbers do you think are probably most accurate?

**b.** If you wanted to round the data so you could make quick comparisons of size, what rounding would you use in each column? Why?

**10.** To make sense of the war data used in questions 1–7, you may find it helpful to compare the numbers with more familiar data.

    **a.** Find the three wars in which the greatest number of people served. Use the table on page 27 to find metropolitan areas and cities with populations approximately equal to the number of people serving in these wars.

    **b.** Armies are usually made up of young people. Find out the number of students in the senior class of your community high school. Then, find the number of senior classes of that size needed to equal the 8,744,000 people who served in the Vietnam War.

**11.** A news report about lottery winnings stated, "Saturday's $43 million Lotto Jackpot equals a trail of $1 bills that would stretch 4100 miles, from New York City to San Francisco and back to Glacier National Park in Montana."

Glacier National Park, Montana

New York City

San Francisco

    **a.** A $1 bill is about 6 inches long. How many $1 bills are needed to make a trail 1 mile long?

    **b.** How many $1 bills are needed to make a trail 4100 miles long?

**12.** Look at the "Other deaths" column in the table of war data for questions 1–7.

    **a.** What might cause "other deaths" during a war?

    **b.** What might explain the changing proportion of "other deaths" to "battle deaths" from the Revolutionary War through the Persian Gulf War?

**13.** This table shows 1987 data for ten countries. For each country, the table gives the number of people serving in the military and the total population. Notice that the numbers of people in the military are given in thousands. For example, the number of people in the military in China is $3530 \times 1000 = 3{,}530{,}000$. The populations are given in millions. For example, the population of China is $1070 \times 1{,}000{,}000 = 1{,}070{,}000{,}000$.

| Country | Number in military (thousands) | Population (millions) |
|---|---|---|
| People's Republic of China | 3530 | 1070 |
| Cuba | 297 | 10 |
| India | 1502 | 790 |
| Iraq | 900 | 17 |
| Israel | 180 | 4 |
| North Korea | 838 | 21 |
| Soviet Union | 4400 | 284 |
| Syria | 400 | 11 |
| United States | 2279 | 245 |
| Vietnam | 1300 | 64 |

Source: *The World Almanac and Book of Facts 1992.* New York: Pharos Books, 1991.

**a.** Which of the countries listed have the greatest and least populations, and what are those populations? Write your answers in *standard notation*. That is, show all the places of each number. For example, the population of Cuba in standard notation is 10,000,000.

**b.** Which of the countries listed have the largest and smallest military forces, and what are the sizes of those military forces? Write your answers in standard notation.

**c.** Which of the countries listed have the greatest and least percents of their population serving in the military, and what are those percents?

**14.** In Problem 3.4, you looked at the 15 North Carolina counties with the largest 1993 hog populations. The bar graph below compares the total hog population of these counties with the total human population of these counties for every even year from 1984 through 1994. How do you think the 1995 hog population compared with the 1995 human population?

**Hog Boom**

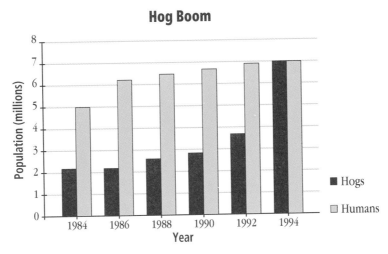

**15.** The table below shows the change in the "hog inventory" from 1993 to 1994 for the five North Carolina counties with the highest 1994 hog populations.

   **a.** If the percent change for each county was the same from 1994 to 1995 as it was from 1993 to 1994, how many hogs were in each county in 1995?

   **b.** Use the information in the table to figure out what the hog inventory for Bladen County was in 1993. How does this number compare with the total 1993 hog population of Bladen County given in the table in Problem 3.4?

| County | 1994 hog inventory (millions) | Growth from 1993 |
|--------|------------------------------|------------------|
| Duplin | 1.47 | 41% |
| Sampson | 1.45 | 26% |
| Wayne | 0.41 | 23% |
| Bladen | 0.41 | 50% |
| Greene | 0.28 | 22% |

Note: The hog inventory is the number of hogs and pigs on farms as of December 1, 1994.
Source: North Carolina Department of Agriculture.

# Extensions

In 16–19, a number in the given statement has been rounded from its actual value. Give the greatest and least possible actual values for the number.

**16.** The longest traffic jam of all time was 110 miles long (rounded to the nearest 10 miles).

**17.** The longest bridge in the United States is the Second Lake Pontchartrain Causeway in Louisiana. It is 125,000 feet long (rounded to the nearest 5000 feet).

**18.** In 1991, there were 50 million (rounded to the nearest 10 million) pet dogs in the United States.

**19.** As of 1989, the United States had the greatest number of telephones of any country in the world, 120,000,000 (rounded to the nearest 10,000,000).

# Mathematical Reflections

In this investigation, you compared, ordered, and rounded large numbers. These questions will help you summarize what you have learned:

1. Describe several ways you can compare large numbers. Be sure to discuss percents, differences, and ordering.

2. Tokyo-Yokohama, Japan, is the most populous city in the world with 28,477,000 residents (as of 1995). How would you round this population to the nearest ten million? To the nearest million? To the nearest hundred thousand? Choose one of these three roundings, and describe a situation in which it would make sense to use this rounding. Explain your reasoning.

3. Describe some ways you could compare the population of Tokyo-Yokohama with the population of the largest metropolitan area in the United States.

   Think about your answers to these questions, discuss your ideas with other students and your teacher, and then write a summary of your findings in your journal.

# How Many Is a Million?

**Y**ou have seen that it is sometimes difficult to get a sense of just how big a large number really is. In previous investigations, you developed some benchmarks to help you imagine large numbers. In this investigation, you will develop a sense of how many a million is. You will also learn a shorthand notation for writing large numbers.

## 4.1 Thinking Big

Large numbers appear in newspaper, radio, and television reports every day.

### The Daily Gazette

| VOL. CXXXIV NO. 24 | FRIDAY, MAY 23, 1997 | ★ ★ ★ ★ |

#### Hog Lagoon Spills a Million Gallons of Waste in Creek!
#### Fish Kill Expected to Run into Millions!

How many is a million? This problem will give you a sense of what a million "looks like."

### Problem 4.1

For each part of this problem, explain how you arrived at your answer.

**A.** How long does it take your heart to beat 1,000,000 times?

**B.** Advertisements for a popular brand of chocolate chip cookie claim that there are 1000 chips in each bag of cookies. How many bags would you need to have 1,000,000 chips? If one bag measures 20 centimeters by 12 centimeters by 6 centimeters, would all of these bags fit in your classroom?

**C.** If someone is 1,000,000 hours old, what is his or her age in years?

**D.** How many students can stand inside a square with an area of 1,000,000 square centimeters?

■ **Problem 4.1 Follow-Up**

Write another question you could ask to help someone get a sense of how many a million is.

### 4.2 Thinking Even Bigger

The questions in Problem 4.1 helped you get a sense of how many a million is. But what about a billion or a trillion? How can you make sense of newspaper headlines like these?

## The Daily Gazette

VOL. CXXI NO. 7                    THURSDAY, OCTOBER 2, 1995                    ★ ★ ★ ★

### U.S. Debt Nears $5 Trillion

### Population of India Passes 1 Billion

### Did you know?

The words *billion* and *trillion* do not mean the same thing in Great Britain as they do in the United States. In the United States, when we say "a million," "a billion," and "a trillion," we mean these numbers:

1 million = 1,000,000
1 billion  = 1,000,000,000
1 trillion = 1,000,000,000,000

In Great Britain, a million is 1,000,000, as it is in the United States, but a billion is 1,000,000,000,000—the number we call a trillion. And a trillion is 1,000,000,000,000,000,000.

In this problem, you will try to imagine a million, a billion, and a trillion as collections of unit cubes. To start, you can line up ten unit cubes to form a *long*. You can then put ten longs together to make a *flat*.

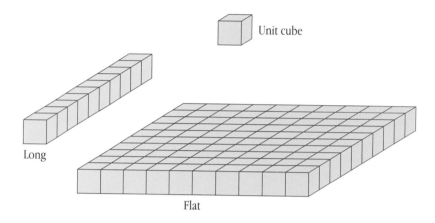

Unit cube

Long

Flat

## Problem 4.2

**A.** How many unit cubes are needed to make one *flat*?

**B.** You can stack ten flats to make a *super cube*. How many unit cubes are needed to make a super cube?

**C.** You can line up ten super cubes to make a *super long*. How many unit cubes are needed to make a super long?

**D.** You can put together ten super longs to make a *super flat*. How many unit cubes are needed to make a super flat?

**E.** You can put together ten super flats to make a *super-duper cube*. How many unit cubes are needed to make a super-duper cube?

### ▪ Problem 4.2 Follow-Up

**1.** How many unit cubes would it take to build a *super-duper long* (made of ten super-duper cubes)? What are the dimensions of a super-duper long?

**2.** How many unit cubes would it take to build a *super-duper flat* (made of ten super-duper longs)? What are the dimensions of a super-duper flat?

**3.** How many unit cubes would it take to build an *extra-super-duper cube* (made of ten super-duper flats)? What are the dimensions of an extra-super-duper cube?

**4.** Which of the super, super-duper, or extra-super-duper arrangements contain more than a million unit cubes? More than a billion unit cubes? More than a trillion unit cubes?

## 4.3 Using Scientific Notation

Numbers used in scientific work are often very large. For example, there are about 33,400,000,000,000,000,000,000 molecules in 1 gram of water. There are about 25,000,000,000,000 red blood cells in a human body. According to the big bang theory in astronomy, our universe began with an explosion 18,000,000,000 years ago, generating temperatures of 100,000,000,000° Celsius.

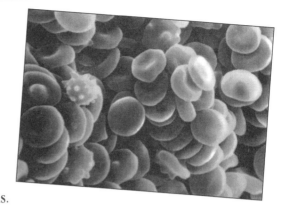

A calculator is a useful tool for working with large numbers. However, to use your calculator effectively, you need to understand the special way it handles large numbers.

### Think about this!

- Try entering 25,000,000,000,000 on your calculator. Does your calculator allow you to enter all the digits? If you are using a graphing calculator, press ENTER after you enter the number. What do you think the resulting display means?

- Use your calculator to find 500,000 × 500,000. What do you think the resulting display means?

- What does the ∧ or $y^x$ key tell your calculator to do?

- Enter 10 ∧ 5, 10 ∧ 8, and 10 ∧ 12 on your calculator (if you are using a nongraphing calculator, you will need to press 10 $y^x$ 5, 10 $y^x$ 8, and 10 $y^x$ 12). What do you think the resulting displays mean?

The product of 500,000 × 500,000 is 250,000,000,000. However, when you tried to compute this product on your calculator, the display probably showed one of these results:

> 2.5E11        or        2.5    11

Your calculator did not make a mistake. It was using a special notation.

To understand your calculator's notation, let's start by looking at a short way to write 100,000,000,000:

$$100,000,000,000 = 10 \times 10 \times 10 \times 10 \times 10 \times 10 \times 10 \times 10 \times 10 \times 10 \times 10$$
$$= 10^{11}$$

In the notation $10^{11}$, 10 is the *base* and 11 is the *exponent.* The exponent tells you how many times the base is used as a factor.

We can use this short way of writing 100,000,000,000 to find a short way to write 250,000,000,000:

$$250,000,000,000 = 2.5 \times 100,000,000,000$$
$$= 2.5 \times 10^{11}$$

The number $2.5 \times 10^{11}$ is written in scientific notation. A number is written in **scientific notation** if it is expressed in the following form:

a number greater than or equal to 1, but less than 10        $\times$        10 raised to an exponent

Scientific notation looks a little different on a calculator. Your calculator was using scientific notation when it displayed

| 2.5E11 |        or        | 2.5        11 |

Both of these displays mean $2.5 \times 10^{11}$.

This example shows how you would use scientific notation to write 4,000,000:

$$4,000,000 = 4.0 \times 1,000,000$$
$$= 4.0 \times 10 \times 10 \times 10 \times 10 \times 10 \times 10$$
$$= 4.0 \times 10^{6}$$

How would your calculator display this number?

## Problem 4.3

**A.** Write each number in standard notation.

    **1.** $10^{22}$      **2.** $10^{13}$      **3.** $10^{11}$      **4.** $10^{10}$

**B.** Write each number in a shorter form by using an exponent.

    **1.** $10 \times 10 \times 10 \times 10 \times 10 \times 10 \times 10 \times 10 \times 10 \times 10 \times 10 \times 10$

    **2.** 1,000,000

**C.** Write each number in standard notation.

    **1.** $3.0 \times 10^9$      **2.** $2.5 \times 10^{13}$      **3.** $1.75 \times 10^{10}$

**D.** Write each number in scientific notation.

    **1.** 5,000,000      **2.** 18,000,000      **3.** 17,900,000,000

**E.** Experiment with your calculator to figure out how to get these displays. Then, write each number in both scientific and standard notation.

    **1.** `1.7E12` or `1.7    12`

    **2.** `1.7E15` or `1.7    15`

    **3.** `2.35E12` or `2.35    12`

    **4.** `3.698E16` or `3.698    16`

### Problem 4.3 Follow-Up

**1.** Look back at your answers for parts C and D of Problem 4.3. Compare the scientific notation for each number with the standard notation. What connections do you see between the two notations?

**2.** Write each of the following as a product of the base, without using an exponent.

    **a.** $10^4$      **b.** $10^7$      **c.** $7^3$

**3.** Describe how you would translate a number written in scientific notation, such as $4 \times 10^{13}$ or $3.5 \times 10^7$, into standard notation.

**4.** Describe how you would translate a number written in standard notation, such as 32,000,000, into scientific notation.

**5.** Write 45,671,234,142 in scientific notation.

As you work on these ACE questions, use your calculator whenever you need it.

# Applications

1.  **a.** Is it possible for someone to be 1,000,000 minutes old? Explain.

    **b.** Is it possible for someone to be 1,000,000,000 minutes old? Explain.

2.  How old would someone be if they were born 1,000,000 days ago?

3.  A typical human heart beats about 70 times a minute.

    **a.** How long does it take a heart to beat 1,000,000 times?

    **b.** How long does it take a heart to beat 1,000,000,000 times?

    **c.** How can you use your answers from parts a and b to figure out how long it takes a heart to beat 1000 times or 1,000,000,000,000 times?

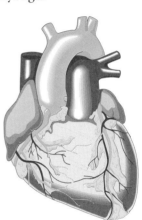

4.  **a.** How many times a million is a billion?

    **b.** How many times a million is a trillion?

    **c.** How many times a billion is a trillion?

5.  The diameter of a penny is about 2 centimeters.

    **a.** How many pennies, laid side by side, would you need to make a line 1000 kilometers long? (Recall that 1 kilometer = 1000 meters and 1 meter = 100 centimeters.)

    **b.** The distance across the United States at its widest point is 3000 miles. How many pennies, laid side by side, would you need to span this distance? (Recall that 1 mile ≈ 1.6 kilometers.)

6.  The population of the world is about 5,700,000,000. Write this number in scientific notation.

**7.** There are about 10,000,000,000 cells in the human brain. Write this number in scientific notation.

In 8–10, use the following table, which shows the monetary cost to the United States of four twentieth-century wars. The figures include the cost to fight the wars and the cost of veterans' benefits paid after the wars.

| War | Cost (dollars) |
|---|---|
| World War I | $6.3 \times 10^{10}$ |
| World War II | $4.48 \times 10^{11}$ |
| Korean War | $6.7 \times 10^{10}$ |
| Vietnam War | $1.67 \times 10^{10}$ |

Source: *The World Almanac and Book of Facts 1992.* New York: Pharos Books, 1991, p. 699.

**8.** Write the costs in standard notation.

**9.** Calculate the total cost of the four wars, and write the result in both scientific and standard notation.

**10.** Which war cost the most? Why do you think this war was the most expensive?

## Connections

**11.** Recall that the *prime factorization* of a number is the factor string made up entirely of primes. One way to find the prime factorization of a number is to make a factor tree. The factor tree at right shows that the prime factorization of 20 is $2 \times 2 \times 5$, or $2^2 \times 5$.

In a–f, write the prime factorization of the number using exponents.

**a.** 100  **b.** 1000  **c.** 10,000

**d.** 100,000  **e.** 1,000,000  **f.** 1,000,000,000

**g.** Look over the prime factorizations you found in parts a–f. What do you notice? Why do you think this happens?

**12.** In a–d, use what you discovered in question 11 to help you find the prime factorization of each number. Write the factorization using exponents.

    **a.** 900

    **b.** 27,000

    **c.** 150,000

    **d.** 24,000,000

**13.** In a–e, use what you discovered in questions 11 and 12 to find each product.

    **a.** $2^2 \times 3 \times 5^2$

    **b.** $2^2 \times 5^3$

    **c.** $2^4 \times 3^2 \times 5^3$

    **d.** $2^3 \times 5^4 \times 7$

    **e.** $2^4 \times 3 \times 5^4 \times 7$

In 14–16, use the following table, which shows trends in the value of records, tapes, compact discs (CDs), and music videos sold from 1975 through 1990.

| Music medium | Value (millions of dollars) | | | |
| --- | --- | --- | --- | --- |
| | 1975 | 1980 | 1985 | 1990 |
| Albums | 1485.0 | 2290.3 | 1280.5 | 86.5 |
| Singles | 211.5 | 269.3 | 281.0 | 94.4 |
| Eight-track tapes | 583.0 | 526.4 | 25.3 | 0 |
| Cassettes | 98.8 | 776.4 | 2411.5 | 3472.4 |
| Cassette singles | 0 | 0 | 0 | 257.9 |
| Compact discs | 0 | 0 | 389.5 | 3451.6 |
| Music videos | 0 | 0 | 0 | 172.3 |

Source: Recording Industry Association of America, as found in the *Statistical Abstract of the United States 1993.* Published by the Bureau of the Census, Washington, D.C., p. 250.

**14.**   **a.** Find the total value of music sold in all media in 1975, and write the result in both scientific and standard notation.

    **b.** Find the total value of music sold in all media in 1990, and write the result in both scientific and standard notation.

    **c.** In a way that makes sense to you, compare the value of music sold in all media in 1990 with that sold in 1975.

**15.** Describe sales trends of various music media that would have helped an owner of a music store predict sales for 1995.

**16.** For each year, combine the data for albums and singles to get the value for all records, and combine the data for eight-track tapes, cassettes, and cassette singles to get the value for all audiotapes. Graph the data for records, audiotapes, and CDs on the same coordinate grid. Describe how the value of each medium changed from 1975 through 1990.

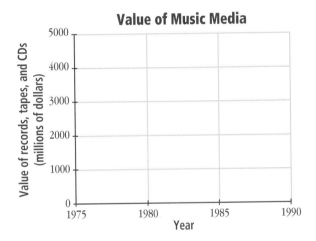

**Value of Music Media**

## Extensions

**17.** **a.** Compute each product mentally.

    **i.** $2000 \times 300$         **ii.** $2000 \times 30,000$

    **iii.** $2500 \times 3000$     **iv.** $15,000 \times 50,000$

  **b.** Describe the strategies you used to compute the products in part a. Can rewriting the factors in scientific notation help you do the mental calculations? If so, explain how.

In 18 and 19, consider the following information*: In the Northwest, some salmon species migrate up to 900 miles from the Pacific Ocean up rivers in the Columbia River basin to spawning streams to lay their eggs. During the 1950s, about 125,000 adult Snake River chinook salmon returned to their spawning streams in the spring and summer of each year. Because of factors such as dam and reservoir construction, the number of salmon that hatch in the spawning grounds, migrate to the ocean, and return to lay eggs has decreased significantly since the 1950s. During the 1980s, an average of 9600 adult Snake River chinook salmon returned to their spawning streams in the spring and summer of each year.

**18.** The table below gives the numbers of adult salmon that returned to their spawning streams each year from 1991 through 1994.

| Year | Number of salmon |
|------|------------------|
| 1991 | 3400 |
| 1992 | 3400 |
| 1993 | 7900 |
| 1994 | 1800 |

**a.** What is the mean number of adult salmon that returned each year from 1991 through 1994?

**b.** What is the average decrease in salmon per year from 1991 through 1994?

*Source: National Marine Fisheries Service

**19. a.** Two adult salmon produce about 4000 eggs, from which about 800 fry, or baby salmon, hatch. Of these 800 fry, about 200 smolts, or young salmon, survive to migrate to the ocean. What is the survival rate of salmon from eggs to young salmon that migrate to the ocean?

**b.** How many eggs must be laid to produce a migration of 1 million salmon to the ocean?

**20.** The table below gives population estimates for major regions of the world. Notice that the estimates are in millions.

| Region | Population in 1995 (millions) |
|---|---|
| Africa | 721 |
| Asia | 3403 |
| North America | 292 |
| Latin America | 481 |
| Europe | 807 |
| Oceania | 29 |

**a.** For each population estimate, tell what your calculator display would look like if you entered the number and pressed ENTER .

**b.** Find the difference between the population of Asia and the population of Africa in two ways: by using the numbers as shown in this table and by first writing the number in standard notation. Explain your results.

# Mathematical Reflections

In this investigation, you developed a sense of how many a million, a billion, and a trillion are, and you learned how to use scientific notation to write large numbers. These questions will help you summarize what you have learned:

1. As you built or imagined larger and larger collections of unit cubes in Problem 4.2, you probably noticed some important connections between numbers.

   a. How many tens are in a hundred?

   b. How many hundreds are in a thousand?

   c. How many thousands are in a million?

   d. How many millions are in a billion?

   e. How many billions are in a trillion?

2. Describe how you can make sense of how many a million, a billion, or a trillion is.

3. When does your calculator display a number in scientific notation?

4. Describe a situation in which scientific notation may be useful.

   Think about your answers to these questions, discuss your ideas with other students and your teacher, and then write a summary of your findings in your journal.

# Every Litter Bit Hurts

**S**ometimes data are reported as *totals*. In Investigation 3, you looked at the total number of people in 20 major metropolitan areas. At other times, data are given as *rates*. In Problem 3.4, you looked at the number of hogs per square mile. In this investigation, you will continue work with data given in both forms, and you will see how you can scale rate data to find useful information.

## 5.1 Going Hog Wild

In Problem 3.4, you looked at data for the 15 North Carolina counties that had the greatest 1993 hog populations. In this problem, you will work with the data from the top 5 counties.

| County | 1993 hog population | Growth from 1983 | Hogs per square mile |
|--------|---------------------|------------------|----------------------|
| Sampson | 1,152,000 | 363% | 1218 |
| Duplin | 1,041,000 | 349% | 1273 |
| Wayne | 333,000 | 265% | 603 |
| Bladen | 271,000 | 1178% | 310 |
| Greene | 231,000 | 82% | 870 |

Source: U.S. Department of Agriculture, as reported in the *Raleigh News and Observer,* 19–26 February 1995.

### Did you know?

- Hogs are one of the most intelligent domesticated animals.
- Hogs have no sweat glands and wallow in the mud to keep cool.
- Hogs weigh about 2.5 pounds at birth. When fully grown, boars (male hogs) may weigh more than 500 pounds.
- Hogs have very poor eyesight but a very keen sense of smell.
- Scientists believe that people began domesticating hogs about 8000 years ago.

## Problem 5.1

Assume the growth of the hog populations continues at the rates given in the table for the ten years from 1993 to 2003.

**A.** Predict the number of hogs in each county at the end of the year 2003. Which counties will have over a million hogs?

**B.** Will the ranking of these five counties be the same in 2003 as it was in 1993? Explain your answer.

### ■ Problem 5.1 Follow-Up

A square mile is about 640 acres. Find the number of hogs per acre for each county in 1993.

## 5.2 Recycling Cans

Do you recycle your aluminum soft drink cans? You might think that recycling the small number of cans you use won't make a difference. But what if everyone reasoned this way?

## Problem 5.2

**A.** Take a class survey, asking each student to estimate the number of soft drink cans he or she uses in a typical week. Make a line plot of the data, and find the mean and the median.

**B.** Estimate the number of cans used by all the students in your class in one day, one week, one month, and one year.

**C.** Estimate the number of cans used by all the students in your school in one day, one week, one month, and one year.

**D.** Estimate the number of cans used by all 260,000,000 Americans in one day, one week, one month, and one year.

### ■ Problem 5.2 Follow-Up

**1.** It takes about 20 soft drink cans to make 1 pound of recycled aluminum. There are 2000 pounds in a ton. Based on your estimates from Problem 5.2, how many tons of recycled aluminum would be produced each year if Americans recycled all their soft drink cans?

**2.** Every ton of recycled aluminum saves 4 tons of *bauxite*, the ore from which aluminum is made. Based on your estimates from Problem 5.2, how much bauxite would be saved each year if Americans recycled all their soft drink cans?

## 5.3 Going Down the Drain

In some countries, droughts make water very precious. In the Middle East and North Africa, water is always in short supply.

Do you leave the water running while you brush your teeth? It may seem that this would not waste much water. In this problem you will investigate how these small amounts of water can add up.

### Problem 5.3

**A.** Time yourself as you brush your teeth, and record the total brushing time. Then, let the water run from the faucet into a large pan for 10 seconds. Use a measuring cup to find the amount of water collected. Use these data to figure out how much water you would use if you let the water run while you brushed your teeth.

**B.** Collect the data for the entire class on the board, and then find the average amount of water used per student.

**C.** Suppose everyone let the water run while brushing their teeth. Estimate the amount of water used by your class for toothbrushing in a typical year. Assume each student brushes twice a day. Extend your estimate to find the amount of water that would be used yearly by all 260,000,000 Americans just for toothbrushing.

### ■ Problem 5.3 Follow-Up

Estimate the amount of water you would save if you used only enough water to wet and rinse your toothbrush and to rinse your mouth after brushing. Compare this figure with the "let it run" estimate you made in part A.

## 5.4 Making Mountains out of Molehills

Soft drink cans are only part of the American trash-disposal problem. Families, businesses, and factories produce many other waste materials. In 1988, the U.S. government estimated that the waste from American households and small businesses or industries, called *municipal waste,* amounts to about 4 pounds per person per day.* This may not seem like much, but remember, there are about 260 million Americans!

### Problem 5.4

Suppose municipal waste could be compacted into cubes measuring 1 foot on each edge. Each such cube would be composed of about 50 pounds of waste.

If all the municipal waste collected from American homes, businesses, and industries were pressed into 1-foot waste cubes, how many cubes would be produced in just one day?

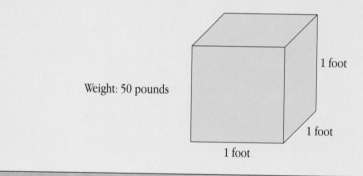

Weight: 50 pounds
1 foot
1 foot
1 foot

### ■ Problem 5.4 Follow-Up

Would the waste cubes produced by Americans in one day fit in your classroom? In your school?

*Source: *Facing America's Trash: What's Next for Municipal Solid Waste?* U.S. Congress OTA. Washington, D.C.: U.S. Government Printing Office, 1989.

As you work on these ACE questions, use your calculator whenever you need it.

# Applications

In 1–4, use the following facts about recycling.*

- People in the United States use about 50 million tons of paper, made from 850 million trees, every year.

- The average household throws away 13,000 pieces of paper each year. Most is packaging and junk mail.

- The Sunday papers published in the United States each week use pulp from 500,000 trees. The *New York Times* alone requires paper from 75,000 trees per week to meet the demands of its Sunday publication.

**1. a.** How many pounds of paper are used in the United States every year? (Recall that 1 ton = 2000 pounds.)

   **b.** What is the average number of pounds of paper used per American each year? (Remember, there are about 260 million Americans.)

   **c.** On average, how many pounds of paper are made from one tree?

   **d.** How many trees does it take to make the paper used per American in a year?

**2.** The 260 million Americans live in 97 million households.

   **a.** What is the average number of people in an American household?

   **b.** How many pieces of paper are thrown away per American in a year?

**3. a.** How many trees are used in one year to make the newsprint for all American Sunday papers?

   **b.** How many trees are used in one year to make the newsprint for just the Sunday *New York Times*?

*Source: Rebecca Stefoff. *Recycling.* New York: Chelsea House, 1991.

# Connections

4. Below is a table of data from a middle school class showing the water used by each student in one week.

**Students' Water Use**

| Student initials | Gallons per student |
|---|---|
| RE | 380 |
| TW | 420 |
| HW | 299 |
| WE | 334 |
| GK | 266 |
| DJ | 218 |
| MJ | 246 |
| WD | 246 |
| MA | 241 |
| LR | 206 |
| FP | 247 |
| HA | 197 |
| TB | 313 |
| CH | 188 |
| ME | 231 |
| JW | 228 |
| PR | 211 |
| NP | 273 |
| BH | 202 |
| EB | 189 |
| PJ | 182 |
| HJ | 160 |
| HM | 185 |
| JZ | 247 |

**a.** What is the median number of gallons of water used in a week by each student? Use this information to estimate the total number of gallons of water used by all 260,000,000 Americans in a week.

**b.** What is the mean number of gallons of water used in a week by each student? Use this information to estimate the total number of gallons of water used by all 260,000,000 Americans in a week.

**c.** How do the mean and median number of gallons used per student compare? Why do you think this is so? How did the difference between the mean and the median affect the estimates you made of the weekly use of water by all 260,000,000 Americans?

**5.** Rabies is a dangerous disease that can infect people and animals. Since 1990, rabies has been found in large numbers of raccoons in the eastern United States. In two counties in New Jersey, the cost of rabies prevention rose from $768,488 in 1988 to $1,952,014 in 1990. In New York State, the number of suspected rabies cases in animals rose from 3000 in 1989 to 12,000 in 1993.

In Europe, rabies in foxes has been controlled by mixing vaccine with bait and leaving the bait for the foxes to eat. In Europe, about 75 million vaccine doses were distributed from 1978 through 1994. Because this method was so successful, it is now being tried with raccoons in the United States.*

**a.** What was the percent change in the cost of rabies prevention from 1988 to 1990 for the two New Jersey counties mentioned above?

**b.** On average, how many vaccine doses were distributed per year in Europe from 1978 through 1994?

**c.** It takes 260 vaccine doses per square mile of land for the vaccine to be effective. If these guidelines were followed in Europe, about how many square miles of land were dosed per year?

*Source: C. E. Ruprecht, et al., "The Ascension of Wildlife Rabies: A Cause for Public Health Concern or Intervention?" *Emerging Infectious Diseases* 1, no. 4 (1995).

In 6–8, use the following table, which gives information about municipal solid waste produced in six U.S. cities.

**Municipal Solid Waste in U.S. Cities, 1989**

| City | Kilograms per day | Kilograms per day per person |
|------|-------------------|------------------------------|
| Austin, Texas | $4.4 \times 10^5$ | 0.9 |
| Chicago, Illinois | $5.5 \times 10^6$ | 1.8 |
| Chattanooga, Tennessee | $7.1 \times 10^5$ | 4.3 |
| Hamburg, New York | $9.9 \times 10^3$ | 0.9 |
| San Jose, California | $1.6 \times 10^6$ | 2.2 |
| Yakima, Washington | $4.1 \times 10^4$ | 0.9 |

Source: *Facing America's Trash: What's Next for Municipal Solid Waste?* U.S. Congress OTA. Washington, D.C.: U.S. Government Printing Office, 1989.

**6. a.** Rank the cities according to the number of kilograms of solid waste produced each day.

   **b.** Rank the cities according to the amount of solid waste produced per person each day.

   **c.** Which measure of solid waste produced seems better for comparing the cities? Explain your choice.

**7.** Write each amount from the "Kilograms per day" column in standard notation and in words.

**8.** Estimate the population of each city.

# Extensions

In 9 and 10, use the following information: Some of the natural resources we depend on, such as trees and water, are renewable or naturally recycled. Others, such as oil, coal, and gas, are not renewable. Some scientists are urging countries that use natural resources heavily to begin programs of conservation. The table on the following page shows 1989 oil consumption in seven major industrial countries.

## 1989 Oil Consumption

| Country | Oil consumed (barrels) |
|---|---|
| Britain (England, Scotland, Wales) | $6.34 \times 10^8$ |
| Canada | $6.431 \times 10^8$ |
| France | $6.774 \times 10^8$ |
| West Germany | $8.315 \times 10^8$ |
| Italy | $7.081 \times 10^8$ |
| Japan | $1.818 \times 10^9$ |
| United States | $6.324 \times 10^9$ |

**9.** What do you think is the best way to compare the oil consumption of the United States with the oil consumption of the other countries? Explain your choice.

**10. a.** A barrel of oil holds 42 gallons. For each country listed, calculate the oil consumption in gallons.

**b.** Find the 1989 populations of the listed countries in an atlas or almanac. Use this information to find the number of gallons of oil consumed per person in 1989 for each country.

**c.** Using your answer to part b, find the daily oil consumption per person for each country in 1989.

**d.** Compare the rate of oil consumption in the United States to the rates in the other countries. Explain any differences you find.

# Mathematical Reflections

In this investigation, you explored data given both as totals and as rates. For example, in Problem 5.1, you worked with the total hog population and with the number of hogs per square mile. These questions will help you summarize what you have learned:

**1** Look back over the problems in this and other investigations.

**a.** Find examples of data that are expressed as totals and examples of data that are expressed as rates.

**b.** When you rank a set of data, does it make a difference whether you use the totals or the rates? Explain.

**2 a.** If you are given a total for some group of people or time period, how do you calculate a rate per person or per shorter time period?

**b.** If you are given a per-person rate or per-time-period rate, how do you calculate the total for a whole group or for a longer time period?

Think about your answers to these questions, discuss your ideas with other students and your teacher, and then write a summary of your findings in your journal.

# INVESTIGATION 6

# On an Average Day

**N**atural disasters and human catastrophes make the headlines in newspapers and on television and radio news broadcasts. But for a majority of people most days are "average" days. In this investigation, you will look at some interesting facts about average days.

The book *On an Average Day in Japan** compares life in the United States with life in Japan. The book contains lots of data about life in the two countries, and you can discover even more information by doing a little arithmetic. Note that this information was collected when the population of the United States was 250,000,000.

## 6.1 Recycling Cans

On an average day in Japan, about 52,055,000 aluminum cans are used. Japan's population of 123 million people recycles 34,356,000 of those cans. In the United States, which has a population of 250 million people, about 93,310,000 aluminum cans are used on an average day, and about half of them are recycled.

---

### Problem 6.1

**A.** How many aluminum cans are *not* recycled in Japan on an average day?

**B.** How many aluminum cans are *not* recycled in the United States on an average day?

**C.** In an average week, how many aluminum cans are used in each country? How many cans are recycled?

---

### ■ Problem 6.1 Follow-Up

A standard aluminum can is about 12 centimeters tall. If all the cans used in Japan on an average day were stacked in a tower, how tall would the tower be in centimeters? In meters? In kilometers?

*Tom Heyman. *On an Average Day in Japan.* New York: Fawcett Columbine, 1992.

## 6.2 Making Comparisons in Two Ways

There are 250 million people in the United States and 123 million people in Japan. The population of the United States is clearly greater than the population of Japan, but how can you describe how much greater?

You could compare the populations by finding a difference. Since $250 - 123 = 127$, the population of the United States is about 127 million greater than the population of Japan.

You could also compare the populations by figuring out how many times greater the population of the United States is. Since the population of Japan is close to 125 million, and since $250 = 2 \times 125$ (or, equivalently, $250 \div 125 = 2$), the population of the United States is about two times the population of Japan.

### Problem 6.2

The following statements give information about life in Japan and the United States. In each case, compare the data for the countries in the two ways described above, and decide which comparison better explains the similarities or differences.

**A.** The average Japanese child spends 275 hours each year playing sports and games. The average American child spends 550 hours each year in these activities.

**B.** The average American has $10,000 in savings accounts. The average Japanese has about $40,000 saved.

**C.** On an average day, Japanese children spend 7 hours in school, and American children spend 5 hours 25 minutes in school.

**D.** The average American makes 200 telephone calls each month. The average Japanese makes 45 calls each month.

**E.** On an average day, 40% of Japanese use public transportation, while fewer than 4% of Americans do.

### Problem 6.2 Follow-Up

What are some reasons people in the United States and Japan might differ in the ways described in the problem?

## 6.3 Comparing by Using Rates

What is the message in the following statement about photography in Japan and the United States?

> Japanese take 714,500,000 pictures every month, and Americans take 1,250,200,000 pictures every month.

You might conclude that Americans take many more pictures than do Japanese, but remember that the population of the United States is about twice that of Japan.

One way to make a fair comparison in this kind of situation is to calculate a *rate*. In this case, you could find the number of pictures taken per person. In Japan, this rate is as follows:

714,500,000 pictures ÷ 123,000,000 people ≈ 6 pictures per person

In the United States, this rate is as follows:

1,250,200,000 pictures ÷ 250,000,000 people ≈ 5 pictures per person

This comparison tells a different story than does the total number of pictures. Although the number of pictures taken in the United States is greater than the number of pictures taken in Japan, Japanese take more pictures per person.

---

### Problem 6.3

The table below gives some data about smoking in the United States and Japan.

| Country | Population | Smokers | Total cigarettes smoked each day |
|---|---|---|---|
| United States | 250,000,000 | 55,000,000 | 1,437,315,000 |
| Japan | 123,000,000 | 33,000,000 | 849,315,000 |

**A.** Compare the number of smokers in the two countries in as many ways as you can. Which comparison do you believe is best?

**B.** Compare the number of cigarettes smoked each day in the two countries in as many ways as you can. Which comparison do you believe is best?

---

■ **Problem 6.3 Follow-Up**

Would you say that smoking is more widespread in the United States or in Japan? Explain your reasoning.

As you work on these ACE questions, use your calculator whenever you need it.

# Applications

In 1–4, compare the given measurements in two ways, and tell which of the two comparisons you think is better.*

**1.** The tallest man in medical history is Robert Wadlow, who was measured at 8 feet 11 inches (272 centimeters) shortly before his death in 1940. The shortest adult in history is Gul Mohammed of Delhi, India. In 1990, he was measured at $22\frac{1}{2}$ inches (57 centimeters).

**2.** The heaviest person in medical history is Jon Minnoch, who reached a weight of 1387 pounds (630 kilograms). Minnoch's wife weighed 110 pounds (50 kilograms).

**3.** In 1960, the U.S. navy submarine *Triton* traveled around the world in 84 days 19 hours. In 1986, Richard Rutan and Jeana Yeager became the first aviators to fly around the world without refueling, taking 9 days 3 minutes 44 seconds.

**4.** The largest hamburger on record was made at a county fair in Wisconsin in 1989. It weighed 5520 pounds (2509 kilograms) and had a diameter of 21 feet (6.4 meters). The largest pizza was baked at a market in South Africa in 1990. It had a diameter of 122 feet 8 inches (37.4 meters) and an area of 11,818 square feet (1098 square meters).

**5.** A NASA space shuttle travels about 30,000 kilometers per hour.

   **a.** How far will the shuttle travel in one day?

   **b.** How long would it take the shuttle to travel to the moon and back, a distance of about 400,000 kilometers each way?

*Source: *Guinness Book of Records 1994.* Ed. Peter Matthews. New York: Bantam Books, 1994.

**6.** A typical human heart beats about 70 times per minute.

    **a.** How many times does a typical heart beat in an hour?

    **b.** How many times does a typical heart beat in a day?

    **c.** How many times does a typical heart beat in a year?

**7.** There are about 3,225,000 12-year-olds in the United States.

    **a.** About how many Americans will celebrate their thirteenth birthday each day of the coming year?

    **b.** How many candles will be needed for all Americans who celebrate their thirteenth birthdays this year if each person has a cake with 13 candles?

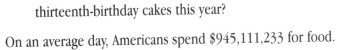

    **c.** If there are 24 candles per box, how many boxes of candles will be needed for all the thirteenth-birthday cakes this year?

**8.** On an average day, Americans spend $945,111,233 for food.

    **a.** How much is this per person per day?

    **b.** How much is this per person per year?

# Connections

**9.** Reports from the Soviet Union, just before it broke into smaller countries in 1991, claimed that on an average day about 70 million Soviet citizens smoked cigarettes at a rate of three cigarettes per smoker.* How many cigarettes were smoked on an average day in the former Soviet Union?

*Source: Tom Heymann. *On an Average Day in the Soviet Union.* New York: Fawcett Columbine, 1990.

**10.** Health researchers estimate that 3 million Americans under age 18 smoke on a daily basis, averaging about 18 cigarettes per smoker per day. How many cigarettes are smoked by Americans under the age of 18 each day in the United States?

**11.** The table below gives the population and land area in 1992 for nine countries.

| Country | Estimated population | Land area (km$^2$) |
|---|---|---|
| Brazil | 150,800,000 | 8,511,957 |
| Canada | 27,400,000 | 9,976,136 |
| France | 56,900,000 | 547,033 |
| Haiti | 6,400,000 | 27,739 |
| India | 882,600,000 | 3,287,591 |
| Nigeria | 90,100,000 | 923,775 |
| People's Republic of China | 1,165,800,000 | 9,596,960 |
| Russia | 149,300,000 | 17,075,352 |
| United States | 255,600,000 | 9,363,109 |

Source: *1992 World Population Data Sheet* of the Population Reference Bureau, Inc.

**a.** Write each number in the table in scientific notation.

**b.** Write the numbers for the least and greatest populations in words.

**c.** Write the numbers for the least and greatest land areas in words.

**d.** When comparing two numbers, is it most useful to write the numbers in standard notation, scientific notation, or words? Explain your answer.

**e.** Divide each population by the corresponding land area to get the population per square kilometer. Then, order the countries by these population densities.

# Extensions

**12.** Try to guess which state in the United States has the greatest population density and which state has the least population density. Then, look up population and land area data in an atlas or other source to check your guesses.

**13.** If you know the population density and land area for a country, state, or city, how can you calculate the population?

In 14–16, tell why the given conclusion is misleading, and explain how you could arrive at a better conclusion.

**14.** On an average day, about 300 Japanese students and about 900 American students drop out of school. *Misleading conclusion:* American students are three times more likely to drop out of school than Japanese students are.

**15.** On an average day, Japanese people make 200 million telephone calls, and Americans make 1800 million calls. *Misleading conclusion:* Americans make about nine times more phone calls each day than do Japanese.

**16.** On an average day, 10,726,000 Japanese travel by subway, and 6,323,000 Americans travel by subway. *Misleading conclusion:* About 1.7 times more Japanese travel by subway than do Americans.

**17.** Use the following newspaper article to answer a–d.

---

### PROBE REACHES JUPITER FOR FIRST CLOSE-UP CONTACT WITH PLANET

After traveling over six years and more than 2,300,000,000,000 miles through space on a data-gathering mission, the *Galileo* spacecraft finally arrived at the planet Jupiter on December 7, 1995. The craft was released from the space shuttle *Atlantis* on October 18, 1989.

A space probe released from *Galileo* on July 13, 1995, slowed from its speed of 106,000 miles per hour as it entered Jupiter's atmosphere, beaming data to the waiting *Galileo* orbiting 133,000 miles above. The spacecraft relayed this infor-mation back to Earth, where scientists received the transmissions roughly 50 minutes after they were sent—the amount of time it takes radio signals to travel the 400,000,000 miles between Jupiter and our planet.

The largest planet in our solar system, Jupiter has a diameter of 88,000 miles, roughly 11 times that of Earth. An average distance of a half a billion miles from the sun, Jupiter takes almost 12 Earth years to make one complete circuit around the sun.

The mass of Earth is 600,588,000,000, 000,000,000,000 short tons. This mass is read as 600 sextillion, 588 quintillion short tons. One short ton is 2000 pounds. ■

---

**a.** Find the average number of miles per day traveled by the *Galileo* spacecraft. How many miles per hour is this?

**b.** At what rate do radio signals travel between Jupiter and Earth? At this rate, how long would it take to send a signal to a spacecraft $1.9 \times 10^{15}$ miles away?

**c.** Write some statements comparing Earth to Jupiter using information from this article.

**d.** Do you think that Jupiter's mass is 11 times Earth's mass? Why?

# Mathematical Reflections

In this investigation, you continued to study data given as totals and as rates. You used ideas from *Comparing and Scaling* to make meaningful comparisons between the United States and Japan. These questions will help you summarize what you have learned:

**1** Look back at your work from this and other investigations. Describe the methods you used to compare two or more numbers.

**2** In a school fund-raiser, students at Hilltop Middle School sold calendars to their friends and families.

**a.** Sales for the sixth grade were $500, sales for the seventh grade were $625, and sales for the eighth grade were $1000. If you were to write a story about the sale for the school paper, what comparison statements could you make on the basis of these data?

**b.** At Hilltop, there are 100 sixth graders, 125 seventh graders, and 100 eighth graders. How would you adjust your statements from part a on the basis of this information?

**3** How do you decide which method for comparing data is best in a given situation?

Think about your answers to these questions, discuss your ideas with other students and your teacher, and then write a summary of your findings in your journal.

# Glossary

**benchmark** A handy reference point to help in understanding the magnitude of other numbers. When working with decimals or fractions, we sometimes use whole numbers and halves as benchmarks, rounding the decimals or fractions to the nearest half. Benchmarks can help us to make sense of the magnitude of a very large number. If the *Exxon Valdez* disaster cost $20,000,000,000 to clean up and the average annual pay for a U.S. worker is $25,000, looking at the number of annual salaries required to pay the cleanup bill can help us to understand the magnitude of this cost. In this example, $25,000 is used as a benchmark.

**customary system** A complex measurement system that originated primarily in the British empire and includes the units of measure inch, yard, pound, and gallon. The system was in use in the United States from the nation's beginnings and is still used today in many situations. In commercial and scientific applications, the metric system is becoming more and more common.

**metric system, international system of measurement, SI system** A measurement system used throughout the world that is based on the powers of 10. The basic units of length, volume, and mass are the meter, liter, and gram, respectively.

**million, billion, trillion** The numbers 1,000,000 (or $10^6$), 1,000,000,000 (or $10^9$), and 1,000,000,000,000 (or $10^{12}$), respectively.

**scientific notation** A short way to write very large or very small numbers. A number written in scientific notation is expressed in this form:

a number greater than or equal to 1 but less than 10  $\times$  10 raised to an exponent

**standard notation** The most common form of written numbers. For example, 254 is the standard notation for 2 hundreds, 5 tens, and 4 ones.

# Index